Martin Luther King Jr.

Civil Rights Leader

by Grace Hansen

ABDO
HISTORY MAKER
BIOGRAPHIES
Kids

abdopublishing.com

Published by Abdo Kids, a division of ABDO, PO Box 398166, Minneapolis, Minnesota 55439.

Printed in the United States of America, North Mankato, Minnesota.

102014

012015

 THIS BOOK CONTAINS RECYCLED MATERIALS

Photo Credits: AP Images, iStock, Landov Media, Shutterstock
© User:Mikefairbanks / CC-SA-3.0 p.5

Production Contributors: Teddy Borth, Jennie Forsberg, Grace Hansen

Design Contributors: Laura Rask, Dorothy Toth

Library of Congress Control Number: 2014943711

Cataloging-in-Publication Data

Hansen, Grace.

 Martin Luther King Jr.: civil rights leader / Grace Hansen.

   p. cm. -- (History maker biographies)

Includes index.

ISBN 978-1-62970-704-4

1. King, Martin Luther, Jr., 1929-1968--Juvenile literature. 2. African Americans --Biography--Juvenile literature. 3. Civil rights workers--United States--Biography --Juvenile literature. 4. Baptists--United States--Clergy--Biography--Juvenile literature. 5. African Americans--Civil rights--History--20th century--Juvenile literature. 1. Title.

323/.092--dc23

[B]

2014943711

Table of Contents

I HAVE A DREAM
MARTIN LUTHER KING, JR.
THE MARCH ON WASHINGTON
FOR JOBS AND FREEDOM
AUGUST 28, 1963

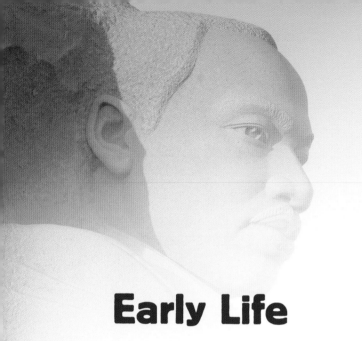

Early Life

Martin Luther King Jr. was born on January 15, 1929. He was born in Atlanta, Georgia.

Georgia

King went to high school

and college. He got his

doctorate in 1955.

Kept Separate

At that time, blacks were not treated the same as whites. The two groups were kept apart. Blacks could not go to white schools. They even had to sit in the back of buses.

Peaceful Protest

In 1955, King led a **peaceful protest**. It lasted for 381 days. No black man or woman rode buses.

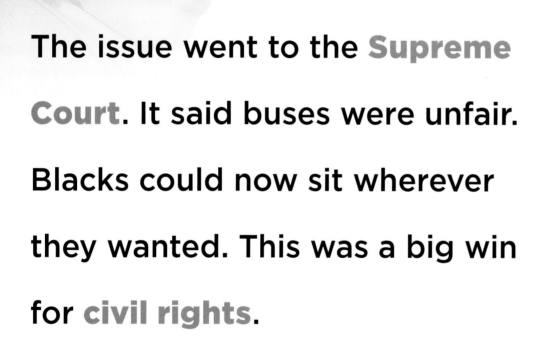

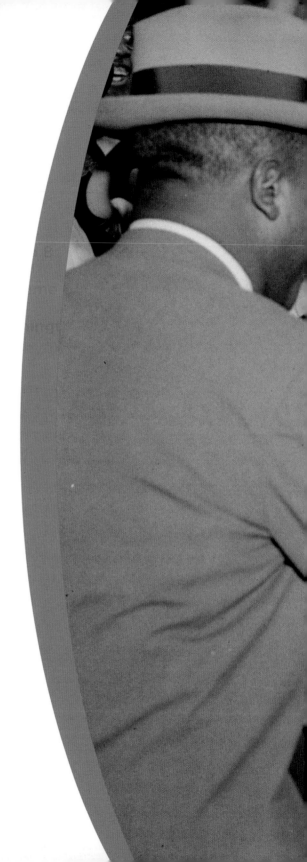

The issue went to the **Supreme Court**. It said buses were unfair. Blacks could now sit wherever they wanted. This was a big win for **civil rights**.

12

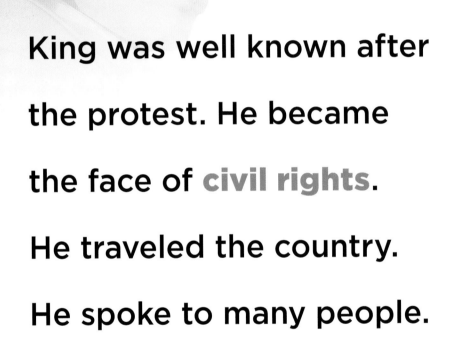

King was well known after

the protest. He became

the face of **civil rights**.

He traveled the country.

He spoke to many people.

"I Have a Dream"

In 1963, King led a peaceful

walk. It was in Washington DC.

Thousands of people came.

He gave his famous

"I Have a Dream" speech.

16

Death & Legacy

On April 4, 1968, King was shot and killed. He was in Memphis, Tennessee.

REV.

THA

MARTIN LUTHER KING JR.

1929 — 1968

FREE AT LAST, FREE AT LAST,

K GOD ALMIGHTY I'M FREE AT LAST

19

King saw a need for change. He made a difference. And he found peaceful ways to do it. He is still remembered as a great leader.

Timeline

King leads a **peaceful protest**. The black community does not ride buses in Montgomery, Alabama, for over a year.

Between 1957 and 1968, King travels more than 6 million miles. He speaks over 2,500 times. He is arrested more than 20 times.

King is the youngest man to receive the **Nobel Peace Prize**.

1955

1957

1964

1929

1956

1963

1968

January 15
Martin Luther King Jr. is born in Atlanta, Georgia.

The Supreme Court rules that separating people on buses by skin color is unfair. King becomes the face of the **Civil Rights** Movement after the ruling.

August 28
King delivers his speech, "I Have a Dream." His dream is that one day all people will be equal.

April 4
King is shot and killed in Memphis, Tennessee. He was leaving his hotel to lead a peaceful march.

Glossary

Civil Rights – a national movement made by black people to gain equal rights and fair treatment.

doctorate – the degree or rank of a doctor.

Nobel Peace Prize – an award given each year to a person who promotes world peace.

peaceful protest – the practice of achieving goals without using violence. King based these types of protests off of things he learned from Christianity and Mahatma Gandhi.

supreme court – the highest judicial court in a country or state.

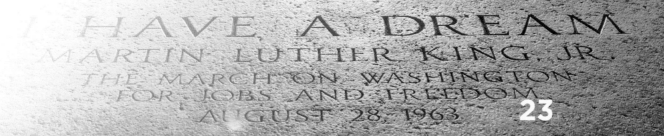

23

Index

abdokids.com

Use this code to log on to abdokids.com and access crafts, games, videos, and more!

Abdo Kids Code:
HMK7044

24